PUNK POETRY

WK LAWRENCE

Broken Tribe Press

PUNK POETRY

BROKEN TRIBE PRESS

Toronto, Canada

Also by WK Lawrence:

State of Love and Trust, 2005
Breathe, Poems for the Planet, 2006
Animals, 2007
Evolution, 2008

Punk Poetry
ISBN: 0692745149
ISBN-13: 978-0692745144

FOR THE PUNKS

PART I PEOPLE WE KNEW

PART II WAR POEMS FROM THE BACK OF THE AMBULANCE

I. PEOPLE WE KNEW

Mythology

Building a bridge, this one strong
        Over water not so troubled,
        A trench of reminders below
        In damp seclusion,
        A bed to visit
        With sheets that slide off
        Into the wind of night
        Like musical notes
        In a cartoon from 1976
        With a cottage on a corner,
        Two doves in the yard,
        A mother and a baby
        Watching him leave for the last time
        With a sac on the back
        Over the bridge
        To the other side of winter
        And that road behind him
        Forever crumbles and falls away
        Into myth.

Purple Toes

I once knew a boy
from the neighborhood
with purple toes
who disappeared
and we all thought he was kidnapped
by a man in a van
because it was the '80s,
before sadistic people
hid behind their computers.

Then I moved to a different town
and met the same boy
with purple toes
all over again.
I assumed he had run away,
but never dared to ask,
nor did he confess,
but he proceeded to show me
his sword collection
and told me how angry he was.

Cold

Red patterns
up, down, and across
swirling in front of my face
like a blinding sun
on a bloated drunken beach
or a kaleidoscope
on a Sunday morning
after too many black eyes.

I hesitate
whether to pick it up
or leave it
with the September rain
where we first met
kissing like romantics under the trestle
of the very train you'd leave on
years later
again in the fall
under gray skies
winter crawling up my knees
the only thing to keep me warm
is this, the sweater you bought me
a final gift I can't bare to accept.

Crazy Johns

There was a kid in my neighborhood
who used to tell me on the street
"I'm gonna tear your face off,"
before he'd chase me for blocks

until I outran him through bushes,
through yards, across busy streets
even when he had the advantage
of being older and having a Mongoose bike,

the one he'd stolen from Danny down the block.

Known by all of us as Crazy John,
he at least had the courtesy
to ask before the chase ensued
whether I wanted it now or later

my face torn off, that is,
and I always answered him
with a scream and a run
as if he were some horror movie monster

and I think we both played into that drama
for how could one really tear a face off
and get away with it, yet be unable to
capture it first.

One day Crazy John just stopped
the violent but ineffective pursuit
and wasn't seen for a while;
rumor was he went away.

I saw him some years later
only once and in passing.
His hair was frayed, eyes red,
and his face didn't look so well.

One-Two-Three

Those grand events in childhood
like the main event on Saturday nights
or the silly Sunday morning show
I'd always wake up early for,
but the grandest were the big ones
once a year every spring
where the drama of months of tension
gave birth to the ultimate feuds
and in a battle of good versus evil
and that one quick move by Benedict Arnold
would result in the fiercest challenge yet
all resolved in twenty minutes
like when Hulk Hogan slammed Andre
or leg-dropped the Macho Man.
Those were moments of triumph and inspiration
all gone and forgotten about
the following weekend
when the wrestling poet arrived
with new poems for the year
printed on Frisbees to throw to the audience
as they await new heroes to fight new villains
in a man's soap opera world of theater.
I respected these wild men
who would scream, sweat, bleed,
and act like children.

Now occasionally,
like a smash into the turnbuckle,

a name pops into my head,
and I Google it to shatter my illusions.
Drugs, death, divorce, suicide, murder,
wheelchair, heart attack, stroke, fat, broke,
washed-up, unskilled, uneducated, sad, mad,
wrestler-turned-preacher,
a universe of utter dysfunction.
Men who spent the better part of their lives
rolling around on a mat in a square ring
roped in from the civilized world.
Those were my heroes for a brief time,
and time is a real life saver.

Diving

A silver and black diver's watch
that my great aunt gave me
on her last Christmas
before the cancer drowned her;
(A final memento of a fine woman
who really cared about the oceans)
stolen from me, my aunt,
now my watch,
taken from my room
by someone with no regard
for the oceans, or any life for that matter,
and certainly no respect for the dead.

Now I can't dive without that watch,
but I guess it's just as well—
Now maybe I won't drown.

Homecoming King

Tall, tan, and handsome,
Dressed, proud, and spoiled,
He looked down on all of us
From a stage
With a banner wrapped around his shoulder—
A crown on his head.

I look back to my yearbook
Or should I say "his book"—
A collage of the best of the homecoming king
With an arm around a pretty girl
On the court shooting hoops
At the prom in a three piece
At rest on a class trip to the beach—
A book of sweet memories.

I think back to the time
I decided to actually run
On the lousy school track
And caught up to the expected winner,
The leader of the race,
The hare, the bully
Who edged me on and screamed,
"Come on, Billy. You think you can run?
You think you can beat me after all of this?"
And I, the tortoise,
Ran past the future homecoming king,
Crossing the finish line—

Humiliation at its best
And I thank him for that gracious moment.

But back to the stage though—
That's all it was—
A place for the scared child to hide
To escape another drunken fight
Between his parents,
Another beating,
Another bed wet,
Another fear,
Another expectation,
Another failure in confidence.

A spectacle he was,
But after a while
The audience slowly disappeared,
And the beer flowed,
The drugs meandered,
And the lights went down.

And he woke up one morning,
a pizza deliveryman.

Driving Her Home

We slept together naked
in the same bed,
but distant in opposing directions
touching only in drifting grazes.

In the morning we awoke
and took a drive through the hills
in circles entangled in the road.
Through trial and error
we found our way
home
to get her bags.

At noon, I drove her to the station
for her five-hour trip home
and even considered
driving her all the way.

Halfway on our voyage
we'd pull over
tired, hungry, craving,
in the middle of the desert,
we'd rent a room to eat, rest...
and well, so we might have considered.

She stepped up,
reached down for one last hug
before disappearing
within the seats of the bus
that took her away
from me.

Wreath

His body is falling and floating away
Sailing off the edge of a bad dream
Climbing through that wreckage
Sawing the rope
Rearranging the mess
Slipping it all around his neck.
It's a quick fall or slow burn.
Which one will it be?

A life in a coma
A page in a lifeless book
A blank picture on a brick wall
A walk down the corridor of cells, of tombs
But it's just as well.
There's no reason to survive, for what?
To pass on the plague?
Black it out. Shut it off. Tune it out. It hurts.
That's the disease that spawns the bullet.
No one's pulled the trigger of his suicide;
They just stepped aside
Under a world of stars falling
Into his lap, burning, sizzling
Through his skin, seeping into veins.
Let it eat away like acid
Or run off into the wild stream
Or drown in the pool
Or in the mouth of those cannibals he calls family
And friends

Stalking him, haunting him—
Those barbarians rip and tear and chew bones
At the fancy dinner table,
A gold table in a wasteland
With holes in the walls around
Because they're cold,
They're jealous,
They're angry.
They've got him bit by bit,
Those selfish assassins,
Devils, tyrants, whatever you call that monster
That steals you from you.

There's no light in this attic
No second chances, no second chances.
No second chance in this life.

Pull Me Under

I gave you my hand.

When I was thrown in the water,
you picked me up and kept me afloat
and punched the ones who tried to drown me.

We swam for awhile
making waves and whirl pools.
Then time passed
and a storm arrived—
the worst storm to hit our lives.
We were young, fragile,
coming from nowhere,
looking for somewhere.

Wind on our face,
waves overhead,
winding down
and wearing us down.

I had grown to be such a strong swimmer
but you,
you had grown tired,
exhausted from the ones
who pulled you in—
friends, family,
for reasons of jealousy,
spite, and well, human nature.

The current grew strong
and you struggled to stay afloat.
I reached out my hand,
but you looked away
off in the distance toward a preserver
that would soon sink
because it was filled with lies and pride.
For it only appeared to be a lifesaver,
like everything else that always appears to be
what it's not.

And so I carry on
without you beside me
walking on solid ground.

Tongue

I once knew a girl
Whose tongue was positioned
So she couldn't stick it out
All the way
But it moved just fine
Just like a normal tongue.
She was my girlfriend's best friend
Until my girlfriend had a fit
Bashing her over the head from behind
Tearing at her long straight brown hair
Dragging her to the ground by her lace
Ripping her clothing away
Pulling at her flesh
Her hips, her legs,
Her freckled back
Gripping onto her
Lashing into her
Until I, grimacing from afar, called for an end.
All that bloody pounding
Just because the friend had said something true
About how she was starting to fall in
With the wrong people.
It shows you, you'd better keep your mouth shut.
Just imagine what she would've done
Had she found out
How I knew about her friend's tongue.

Chemical Wedding

He straps his arm, ties the knot,
taps the vein as he'll soon be wed,
drives it in to ease the hunger—
mouth dry, eyes wet, cold sweat.

The demon intimate with his blood
twists his muscles into mush—
steals his senses one by one.
The ceremony is now complete

but not before one final thought
of sunny days well spent
vulnerable to circumstance
running free and wild.

The smoky room slips away now
like waves on the shore
of a waning beach—
he sees a playground, feels the wind,
hears the children's mad laughter.

Parable of Flight

There is an abundance of personality here,
a diversity of lively souls,
some in need of ablution,
some looking to accelerate
to avoid a belated arrival
to some definitive place;
others belligerent in perspective
even to what is beautiful, even to what is
beneficial,
in a constant breach,
acting and appearing callous
in a world not so candid.

Thinking back chronologically
of all the bad clichés people use,
all the compassion people had and didn't,
the aversions and decisions
that have gradually shaped their demeanors—
some are left with dual lives,
some an enigma
that becomes their own foe;
and I wonder who will endorse them later?
Will they get a fraction of what they deserve?
Will their lives be garnished with love?
I wonder about their habitual problems,
the poor hospitality they've had in some places,
the imperative truth
that we are all so isolated and indifferent at times

always hanging in jeopardy
of falling, yet not seeing the fall,
whether it be emotional, physical,
judicial, or spiritual.

Kudos to their bravery
and to those teachers who will help them
along the way,
so they can think liberally,
and feel spiritually,
and wish for longevity,
and so they can exonerate their loathing
and mementos of their maladies.

A great metamorphosis may come
if only they open their wings.
And they may fly,
be nomadic,
sometimes neurotic,
sometimes quirky,
but they will know the quintessential route
where the view is never obscured,
and where paranoia is obsolete,
and their achievements become paramount
over the synthetic, satirical drama
that life sometimes is.

They've seen the ramifications,
they speak it in their vernacular.

They've lived a tenacious life
one that led to this hopeful renaissance.

And although this world will never be a utopia,
there is a sublime beauty
in the clear blue sky
or the rainy night
or the little wind that visits
from out of nowhere
urging them to be zealous in any vocation
they may choose
and to grow, change, transcend—
fly perpetually, like the birds they are.

The Clumsy Inadequate Professor

Bleeding words
Of another elitist
Ten years spent
On one book
That no one can appreciate
PhD tattoo
Holy now
Am I even worthy enough to be enlightened
Here in this chair, in this room,
By you?
By someone who somewhere along the way
Forgot how to talk to fellow people
Or never knew at all;
Forget about teaching them something,
That holy knowledge
Is too pure to pass along
And they never really show you
What to do with it anyway.
I've listened, I've tried, I've asked for help,
I'm just the kid from the other side of the tracks
Who has already earned my C minus
And already surpassed this chum.

Ride

Slanted light
Accentuated
On her hips
The jury acquits
And we are free, free,
Free of a strident hold
Galloping hard into the sunset
High colors
Fair reasons
An angel coaxed in
For a ride through the country
Breathe easy
Pace yourself, darling
You don't want to run out of fuel
In Kansas
Hold on tight
Don't want to fall off the horse
In Colorado
When we get to the other side of the mountain
Let it break free
And run
Down towards those cushioned puffy clouds
Then we'll pull the world over us.

II. WAR POEMS

FROM THE BACK OF THE AMBULANCE

Recreation

People with arms like levers
With signs in their eyes
Forget all about their time, space,
Homes, families,
All for the thrill of a minute,
While others cozy up in sleeping bags
Filled with nightmares
Deep inside a dark unknown,
As others sing songs
About eating cherries,
Burning Bibles,
Melting ice cream,
And others slip right in
To holes in the ground
Where only echoes can be heard
Coming from the bottom of neutrality.

Rights for Lives

A troop of angels shot
On the moss plagued sidewalk
As streams of red run sideways
Along canyon walls
Flowing around us
We're in the middle
Watching, empty mouthed, waiting
For someone else to do something
For someone else to say something
Like "what the fuck?
Why another killing?
Why another victim for another's privilege?"
But no one says anything
And we all just stare away
Adjusting the circuits
Dusting off the pieces
Sometimes blown to smithereens.

The Decline of Civilization (A Call for Poems)

Can we get one serious poem
out of the poet laureate?
How about suffering
change
death
life
and not about poetry
or a stroll through an elite garden
or some lonely picture in his lonely mind?

How about a poem that calls
people out of their homes
day and night
to listen to the words
to hear justice and freedom
and peace prevail?

How about a sonnet
like a siren
that wakes people from their slumber?

How about free verse
that's really free
that liberates us
and sets loose the wild horses
to stampede the flames?

How about a simple haiku
that ends hunger
and oppression
and gives everyone a home again?

How about a poem that explores the universe
or makes one of its own
and thinks bigger than the unfortunate
lonely little backyard we're all in?

Army Reserve

They're building your prison brick by brick
Drawing lines in the sand
Of sacrificial blessing.

You're floating now
Down the river of no return
Occasionally catching a branch
But eventually continuing on
Until you empty into an ocean
Right into the heart
Of a storm
Like two thousand and one
Summer nights
Lost
Like a dog
Surfing, wiping out
Waking up
On an island
Under a red sky at night.
You take a breath—
It's a great day
To live
Stranded
Alone again
Where the river breaks.

The time has come—
The eyes of the world turn
And you finally put down that weapon.

Document

Spots of darkness
dance before me.
I'm getting tired
but I forge on
trying to capture in pixels
the scene of a crime—
a construction site
of tools used to build
and cover up what once was:
screwdrivers, hammers, bulldozers—
a visual alarm
that sounds a siren far and wide
into night time windows
around a ceiling fan
then blown to crevices
in silent corners
where grandfathers sit
in chairs with leftovers
watching animals on TV
and no one talks.

Billions of Bullets

It's April and raining lead again.
We mourn, bury, and worship the dead
but have we no concept
of the right to really live?

We protect those little boyish ideals
inside their fantasy cops and robbers,
fingers as guns: big bad definition,
prisoner to a false dichotomy.

They call it a sport
but when is death a sport?

Actually, death is very much a sport
in most civilized parts of the world:
athletic leaps and bounds
in chemicals and tastebuds
every time we sit down
every time we indulge
in the rush of speed
or the strategy of lust-ridden desire
just look at
the ways we kill,
the many ways we die—
there are no accidents,
there are no mysteries.

Our hands and one finger
bare
permanent guns.

Finding Things

In the dark crevice of the seashell
The sound of an ocean
A blowing wind   A wave

Rolling in over you
                    Salt in the eyes

Stars overhead
In a kaleidoscope
Of flashes
And explosions   Trampled down
Feeling the low kicks
In the kidneys   Pebbles in your knees
Only patches now

                Fading light
A crime you don't remember
Under a falling building
With the lights still on
Even on the 99th floor

                Beautiful from up there
And down there too
Under the bedrock
Of a past civilization
That also wouldn't remember
How it buried itself   In the sand
Up to the neck
                    Ocean rolling in
A treasure at your feet
        Pick it up, won't you?

Home Invasion

Headlights
Spraying glass
Wood cracking
Wheels spinning
Inches away
From my feet
Up on the coffee table
Back pressed to the sofa
Feeling violated
Steam rising
The engine dies
And I can go back to my nightly trance now.

We'll clean it all up tomorrow.

What If?

Today the dictator was hanged
perhaps rightfully so
for war crimes
of slaughter and torture
and terror by poison.
And it makes you wonder
how the world would have been
if he hadn't been born
if he had had a different childhood
if he had walked a different path—

       Become an artist, perhaps a florist
       and if all those families hadn't been broken
       if all those bodies hadn't been buried
       if all those foreign bullets hadn't been fired
       all those bombs blasted?
       It makes one wonder
       what if?
       what if a U.S. president
       hadn't given him those weapons?

On Line

Absent minded
Days wasted away
In "chat" rooms
Of a virtual reality
On a highway of infinite faith
Where your screen-name
Echoes the primordial conflict of earth
And your profile is of a vacant stare
Trapped emotions screaming
Inside a cauldron
Face to face
With the eyes of the world.

Maturity

Last night I had a dream
I woke up in a fit
and stormed outside to have a smoke
to relieve some inner tension.
I woke up today
wanting a smoke, but haven't had one
in ten months.
And in that time I've given birth
to somebody new
a little fuller
a little healthier
a little lazier too, for some odd reason
I don't clean so much anymore—
The dishes go neglected,
the laundry piles up,
the counter goes wet without a wipe
after the occasional shave
like a man in a coma
whose nurse comes to clean him up
every few days
and whose best friend died
ten months earlier in a night ride
out the window on a highway.

I may never get over this.

Shelter Me

Two weeks worth of coverage and warmth
tumbles in a triple load
suds slushing against glass
round and round, the dirt washes away.
All colors, whites too,
in a segregated machine of course,
underwater drowning
together anyway
but suddenly there's a rapid spin,
the water drains
and it is time to dry.
Now they go around in large swoops
crashing down into each other
two weeks worth of warmth
now warm as an oven
baked and ready to go
for another two weeks of cover.

Allies and Enemies

It'll always be this way
because we set up a game
of absolutes
apples or oranges
cat or dog
bird or mouse
hot or cold
winter or spring
lover or luster
friend or foe
good or evil
either or
lose one
gain another
.

The Witches

In the early twentieth century
we were conditioned to accept a day
of excess and gluttony based on a conjured up
birth date of a man
who would've been horrified
to see what has become a celebration in his name
helped along with the lie we tell children
about a character created by a cartoonist.

Today, they celebrate a man
they still don't understand.
No, they merely celebrate a slogan,
some institution under a steeple conjured up
to control, blind, silence freedom and thought.

And so they celebrate a man whose name
has been smeared
in the mud of centuries long festivals of sin
filling their homes with greed,
their bellies with gluttony,
murdering innocence,
lusting their neighbor's wife or child.

These are the twelve days of sloth
and to question them
will find one in the grasp of wrath, oh tradition!
No different than the witching den,
the clan, the terrorist cell,
a cult, an array of marching believers believing
only what they're told,
and quite proud to do so.

The Way of the Ages

Figure skating our way
To adulthood.
Whose fault
Is it that humanity
Lost a battle in Eden
Under some moonlit moment
Of denial?
Bloody denial
Where she saw him
Under a blanketed sky
Of virginity
Alone
To rot
In a dirt grave
Near frozen
Like an angel in the snow
Near a lake
Where in silence, a child
Slips one foot into her skates.

Whipping

Ankles strain
on this rocky path
as he comes upon a whip
from an ugly past.

Blood still wet
melting into dirt
that will grow
poisonous crops tomorrow.

He continues on
up the hill
until he comes upon
a wooden box still

empty inside
except for a book
with words that kill,
brag, blind, and boast.

As he travels on, it's steep
and the goat beside him
has fallen aside, asleep
broken at his expense

so he lets her rest
and goes on alone
to fight his own battles
on this familiar hill

and when he arrives
it is cold and desolate.

Peering over the edge
he sees they're still at it,
hurting,
hating,
whipping.

A Storm in July

I saw a thousand blinding flashes,
it could've been a war—
another government dropping bombs,
and it was an authority,
but not the one we usually adhere to.

On the hottest day of the year
a great storm struck at night
blowing in from nowhere
and then blowing out.

In that one hour
we saw what could have been the end
of mass suffering— War, lies, greed.
It could've been the beginning of something
beautiful.

Fierce winds rattled the shingles,
angry hail pattered the windows like fingers,
trees crackled and lightening crashed
and every second felt like a minute.

When the long hour was done
and the winds slipped away
I stuck my head outside
to peak at the damage,
but somehow, everything looked better.

We lit candles, relieved to have our world back
for at least a little while
before the TVs returned
to suck in our fellow humans.

For now, it was black
and the traditional power was out,
but we felt powerful
in the candlelight.

We watched the retreating flashes
as the purple sky hypnotized us
and then another loud bang
snapped us back into a comfortable place
we haven't been in a long time.

Brutal Origins

Man cuts another's throat
in the parking lot after work—
now he's the top guy at the office.

Woman pushes another down the stairs
and blames it on her heels—
now she's at the top of the stairs.

Humans push other species
into near extinction
with pollution, poaching—
all to be on top.

Male animals battle
to be the one to mate
with waiting female—

Only one top spot.

Sperm battle inside
to the end of the canal
to the beginning of something familiar,
something beautiful but fierce,
the top spot made for one,
sometimes two, or three, or more,
but mostly just one.

Crux of Centuries

An electric guitar
plugged in
to a hill
an ancient coliseum
reflected.
She arrives
picks up the instrument
plays the sounds of centuries
screeching screams
bellows of oppression
from the core of her soul.
The ground rumbles
the walls collapse
the birds scatter
and she has risen
to the occasion.

Holidays

Goodbye October
Time to get the decorations out
Skip right past Thanksgiving
Like one skips the mourning
Of someone they despise
Move right to the presents
To the toys parents kill each other over
And then blame the chaos
On a fat white bearded man
Who drank all the milk
Ate all the cookies
And left all of the crumbs
That children will celebrate.
Yet another successful year.

New Years

On Christmas Eve
I had too much white wine
because people kept refilling my glass
before it was even half empty.
Then I had a couple glasses of red;
that's when the queasiness set in
around midnight
when children are settling in
or tossing and turning
restlessly waiting for the Santa they worship
while I had a different kind: porcelain worship
some of them will grow up to know quite well.
This is where the whiplash occurred
and where I made a holy mess
of that elegant room
with locked door
and people shaking the knob—
cookies for Santa and everyone else too.
The next day my neck was sore
and my head started to fill
with all the illnesses of the year
which I tried to explain to my wife
but it was useless—
to try and detail the various inflictions
where they come from
and where they're going.
The sickness began to seep out
of various passages
of my puffy face in wretched pain
and on January first, it was time to start
all over again.

Lack of Understanding

An axe
Cuts into wood

A bridge
Connects the land

Grind one
Burn another
But never understand
Why you drown in open spaces.

The Jungle

The males licks the baby male
and its baldness
one final goodbye
one the child will not remember
before the elder goes off
on another path
leaving the baby
inches away from the teeth of danger
of being eaten
in a harsh world
by the iron jaws of life
but this baby makes it—

The mother is strong
and he learns to be like her
until the day he too sets off
leaving the mother as the elder did
at some place along the trail
but yet not quite the same way.

The elder and son travel
parallel
but the elder's forest is barren
and grows hot and inhospitable
and fades into hostile jungle
with a sand that slowly
sucks the elder in
and the last thing he sees
before the sand closes his eyes
is his son traveling the higher road,
the smarter road, and he is proud
but sorry that he rushed ahead.

III. THE AMERICAN DREAM

WK LAWRENCE

Dreams

Jimmy dreams of a big, square, red house
surrounded by sunflowers
only a drive away
from waterfalls and mossy streams.

He wants to take that drive
everyday to work
to photograph the scenery,
film some animals too
in motion
Living
Breathing
maybe even dying.

"But who's going to pay me for my work,
a middle class boy like me?
I've got bills to pay,
places to conquer,
status to buy."

So he gets a job in sales,
buys a big, square, red house
surrounded by sunflowers
only a drive away
from the guy who sacrificed
and lives
and breathes
someone else's dream.

The Last Train

The last train just stopped
And the ad machine just jammed
No more advice from Madison Ave
No more anxiety from the terror squad
No more diarrhea from the doctors
No more nausea from the preachers
Who poison our minds
Poison our food
Poison our souls
Just so we pop their pills
Of propaganda.

Well, the church of pharmaceuticals just burned
And the roof caved in too.
The hoses of truth
Have flooded the entire city
Even the floor of the Capitol
Where our Congress is running for their lives
And they've just found out
Their life preservers are fake.
They never learned to swim
And even if they could
Their metal hinges have rusted tight
With no oil left.

A public veto.

A Journey

Tar under the wheels
Blurring past yellow lines
Crossing bridges
Back onto main land
Tall shadows of concrete and steel loom behind
As the trees sprout up
Replacing those shadows
Ancient bedrock exposed
Up and down the landscape
A warm up in elevation for later
Soon it's all flat again
Corn husks blowing by our faces
Sky turns gray and swirling
And we can almost see a little boy
With a feather in his ear
Sitting upon a hill with a bison by his side
And for a while these wheels turn into hooves
And the tar turns to dirt
Only the growing elevation pulls us back
To a world behind a windshield
Sweating, straining, burning more fuel
Snow begins to pelt the glass
And it looks like we're flying through space
Stars rushing by as we come off that mountain
Tall shadows of snow capped majesty looms
As trees sprout again
We travel parallel to a gorge
In and out of a valley
Through the rain, the wind, and blue
To the ocean and we don't stop.

Turbulence

Shaking side to side
up then down
through a patch of gray
and then a darker patch
of black with white flashes around—
a storm that has potential
of plucking me from flight
and depositing me in the sea of lost lives
or a far worse fate
of scattered ashes and smoldering blackness.

A familiar woman
with blond hair in a bun
a nice little face
and proper attentiveness
offers me a drink
to stray my mind
from the consequences
and I accept her offer.

It's a rare occasion, of course
but it is a chance
we all take just to break away
from where we're from.

And I'd do it all over again.

Bass

A five-hundred-dollar ghetto car
with a two-thousand-dollar stereo
rolls down the street
rattling our windows with its bass.

How it must feel inside
that hollow gangsta head
to crave a constant pounding
of the brain over and over

until the driver is a driving zombie
and the passenger a vegetable
already given a headstart
with the cell-slicing smoke

of an ash tasting blunt
rolled on the dashboard
of a rolling five-hundred dollar casket
and we hear their open booming heartbeat

Can you hear it?
that self sadism
exploding into premature cardiac arrest
and then the pick hitting the ground
digging the grave

                        fading bass.

TV Blues

Are you tired
of everyone selling something?
Something you don't want
Something you don't need
Something you don't believe:
A god that needs cash,
Jesus, Allah, senseless opposition,
terror color codes— a game of Twister,
weapons that didn't exist,
government failures that did,
fudged over with excuses,
Hypocrisy.
Fashion and vanity too—
a new plastic face,
Botox injections in the brain,
the latest quick-fix fad diet
that never works,
dead animal on a plate,
chemicals in what you ate.
SUV's to fog the sky,
more drugs to jog the mind
into a side-effect frenzy
of dissatisfaction, nausea, diarrhea, headaches,
sexual malfunction, mental breakdown.
We'll thank the happy pills
that didn't really make you happy,
only made you forget for a little while—
denial, the way of the world
all sold to you via direct satellite
on your brand new 60 inch wall screen
where you learned to live
and found your morals in a reality TV re-run.

The Last Night of an Old Day

My car is bright in the moon
as you and I fly in this glowing night.
I lean back, stretch my neck, arch my back,
adjusting my eyes to water beading off the
windshield.

Occasionally we strike a lake of a puddle
and as it pulls the wheel one way
I resist holding it steady
letting out a loud "whoa there."

And we drive all night,
the sun rising slowly behind us
on an early summer morning
as the rain recedes to light.

Cities and cornstalks behind us,
we climb the Rocky Mountains
filling our lungs with pine and spruce
knowing paradise is just on the other side.

One more dusk until dawn,
the last of a late mountain snow;
a thousand lights flashing before our eyes;
if we get through this, we'll be fine.

I'd Rather Starve

Ron the clown
I want to take him out back
And kick his ass
Along with every other clown
But Ron's the worst
Worse than the ones who ruin birthday parties
Worse than the ones who corrupt schools
A little worse than the ones at the circus.
Ron is the worst
Because he sells death to kids
On a bun
Poison on a plate
Profit in the pockets
Pompous corporate pride.

How that must feel
To get up in the morning
Put those feet into that red striped suit
And set out for a day's work
Just to put food on the table.

Too Close

Three hikers
sitting on a log for a breather
and it can't distinguish them
from hunter with rifle.

A feast for an entire family
or a trophy above the fireplace
if games were allowed in this park
but they're not.

And those hikers
are mere spectators
in a forest where they too once belonged
long ago
before man needed metal to feel good,

when he still lived in harmony with the forest
before all those dwelling there
knew what they know now,
not to get too close.

Grace

Another harmonized rendition
Face on the wall
Horizon landscape
Of an alternative Monday
Where there are no bouts of mania
Scars are erased
One dot at a time
In a jetting motion
Hard
Like a jack rabbit
Frolicking, escaping
The savage hands
Of grace.

Invisible Humpty Dumpty

Sing the diary by your side out-loud
Tell the world your pipedreams
And watch those flowers grow
In the window of your cage
Safely following the light
Of the last night train
In an afterglow smile
That makes the indefinite stay worthwhile.

In and Out

The pipes fill with oil
on the first cold night of the year,
frost on the window, force on the wrist,
the dog is barking at the pipes.

Where is that dog all day long?
When invaders call and visit
inviting themselves over whenever they choose.
It makes me want to bite the mailman

because I can't get any peace
to put together a creation
and hold a cohesive thought
long enough to construe a truth.

So I take a run
through my unfulfilling neighborhood
past the house where I dreamt
a woman seduced me on her couch

in the middle of the day.
She pulled me indoors
as I was walking the dog,
which of course never happened,

but nevertheless there's her yellow house
as I run past it like Ned,
except I'm not swimming
in a bottle of booze.

I'm just running—
breath, heels, blisters, and suburbia

Here I go until I reach the woods—
not the ones Goodman Brown lurks in,

Not the ones the Igbo toss their twins to—
this forest is all peace
except for the remnants of people
here and there with no explanation of origin.

Like the old Remington I find
frozen in the yellow leaves,
a little rusty around the edges,
but I bet those keys still type.

Who would throw away such an ancient relic?
Was it Kerouac trying to undo what he
attempted?
Was it Burroughs guilty of his addictions?
Or Kafka guilty of his lust or lack of?

Ah, why bother? I'll never know.
So I run on through the woods
past crumbled foundations of brick—
a city lost and overgrown

with ideologies that belong only in books
and divisive fallacies like "us or them"
yet the people knew the truth—
they just couldn't face it—

for the truth will make you go hungry
if you know where your food really comes from.
It'll make you starve or crave
the inner peace of a brontosaurus

where the savages are all one
and the scapegoats are none
and we think it and breath it
and watch it grow— now that is progress

where war is bankrupt
and hate is myth
and greed is obsolete
and money is funny

but this city didn't starve.
No, this city ate and ate and ate
like Romans in the palace
until it was so full and sick that is burst

but that's that city, or at least it was.
Now it's dust and bones
and I'm out of the forest.

Ghosts

Can you see the ghosts?
Upon their arrival to the subway
underneath the business, the crime, the drama
where tyrants once ruled
before they had 70th floor mahogany offices.

The natives all gnashing their teeth
planning their relentless revenge
on a civilization and its venomous leaders
for desecrating their treasures
and building over their pleasures.

The colonists alike nod their heads
confident now, they shake hands
with a mutual regret
for their achievements and losses,
greed and foolishness.

They head upstairs to the streets on a mission
to spook people
who don't see their treasure for what it was—
the bankers, the brokers, the appraisers,
the builders—
they all feel something on their shoulders—
a tap, a scratch, a poke, a hand.
They all turn to find no one
in a blindness that lives on.

Sales

Yesterday someone knocked on my door
from the cult of people.

They were looking to sell soul
but I know what it really was.

They persisted with narrow hallways,
labyrinths with creatures,
shiny apples,
chiseled surfaces,
gloomy endings,
enameled oceans.
What a narrative!
What a show!
And when it concluded
they wanted money
on a continual basis
for a bargain basement idea
a drunk man could've concocted
at 2:30 in the afternoon.

Go sell your stories somewhere else—

We've already heard them a million times.

IV. MORE PUNK PROTESTS

WK LAWRENCE

Window to the West

Eggs unbroken
Frail cut grass
Trees coming into leaf
Like something
Recently said
Lingering in the back
Closets of your mind
Where pilgrims of memory
Huddle
Waiting for a shrine
To exemplify these fields
Where nomads once died
On their way to a birth
Of a silence, a stillness,
A background of someone's photograph
Hundreds of years later
Still under the same moon
Still teetering on the edge
Of an unforgiving sea
Hearing the echo of time
In the coal fire of solitude.

What Once Was

Trees, the ones that are left
sway with the wind,
one here, one there
scattered around the side of the road
outside the front of the shopping mall,
the one named after the old bearded man.

Inside the concrete and steel
one can find their luxuries (and some necessities?)
everything they might want—
clothes, jewelry, massage chairs, junk,
everything except *Leaves of Grass*.
For that, you need to cross the highway
named after the old bearded man
over four lanes of smoggy traffic
to the other side where there are more stores,
even an optometrist
to help you with what you're seeing.

Behind these merchants is the birthplace,
the one the old bearded man's father built
with his bare hands,
where his mother gave birth
to greatness in the main room.
The house is restored now and safely hidden
away from the traffic and capitalism.
It stands alone among all the congestion,
another world fenced in by tall barriers.

Further on west past the house
and through a neighborhood of homes
there's an entrance to a path

that leads into the forest,
Behold! There is still forest here!
At least there are pockets of it anyway
here and there scattered around suburbs.
The path takes us to the top,
the highest point on the island
where he once stood and sat
and loved the land
and wrote of it in pages and pages of admiration.
On top now there is a rock
with his verse engraved into it
for all to remember what once was.

Though if you travel back down the path,
through the neighborhood,
past the old fenced-in home
and the stores that now line the road
named after him,
you can sometimes see him,
an old bearded man,
sick and tired,
sometimes sitting on the curb
with his head down,
sometimes sick on the sidewalk,
trying to hold himself up,
swearing obscenities,
disappointed in the world.

And if you happen to see him,
you are one of the few who remembers
what once was.

Closed

These are the vapors around the rising sun—
The common man that opens learning eyes.
The strong rise on what the weak rely on
Until they speak with new leader high
Above with the great spirit on his side
And victory follows upon our time
Of world peace and unity
And we have made greatness our companion
Until the hourglass is once again flipped
When the common man closes his eyes to the sun.

We Like Where He Stands

We stop on the steps of city hall
holding hands
as protestors chant
and stand their ground
for the impoverished homeless
who freeze to death
on January nights
because politics ignore them.

We pause a moment
before heading in for our license
to love
and then proceed past the spectacle,
only to glance back over
our shoulders
at the man dressed in black
with a white collar—
shouting, praying, pounding
on a brown coffin
he wheeled up onto the sidewalk.

In seven months he'll marry us.

Survivor

The thunderous fire in the sky
lights the dark sand beneath
where something feels
as if it's gone adrift,
as if we've traveled too far
to ever turn around.

These papier-mâchés keep showing
up here and there,
while my mechanical friends
question my very breathing existence
with instructions on the intercom

are breaking me down now
like Vietnam.
They pull at my black boots
with persistence
and resist— I try to,
but they pound and pound
their words, their sticks, their stones,
they're breaking bones.

They prop me up for the holidays
and keep me here
even though I want to go
and meet my maker
to tell the cruel joker
how it feels to be a soldier.

A Machine that Runs

Oil drips
Into parts
That run the machine—
Sloshes around
And lubricates
To solve all of our problems
Or so we thought.

Eventually
Machinery wears
And oil leaks
And metal grinds
And wires short
Causing flood and fire,
Blood and famine,
Perpetual war.

Bright orange blast
And everything that wears is gone.
Only the cockroach survives
In a soup of Creamsicle stew
Where years later
A blade of grass sprouts again
But we sure as hell don't.

So let's go ahead
And extrapolate
What started this all.

#65, 2003, USA

Awaiting my toxic death I hold my breath;
The guards arrive to my cold cell
of iron and rock and windows of black.

Chains dangle with every step,
and I don't remember the day
they say I stole a life away.

In the white room they remove the chains
and I lay down like I did when I used to get hit.

A guard straps me in and touches my wrist
the way the stranger did before he licked.

The priest says a prayer like my defense:
a whiskey soaked lawyer,
the outcome makes no sense.

The blindfold comes down
and seals my tomb,
dark like the closet I used to hide in.

Prick.

Chemicals invade,
now here I am again
just where I began

full of blood inside
the womb.

Blindness spreads.

Sure Is

The breath of a scream
on my nose
fogged my glasses
and pushed me over
but I fought back
with persistent vehemence
until the fingers
started poking
and the hands
started shoving
and they said I'm the one
who's wrong.

I fall over again
into a hole
where there's no fighting
or talking back,
but there sure is democracy.

Kite

The neighborhood went black
one summer night
and we all had the stars back
to light our way
and we all had the car radios back
to tell us the news
so we waited and listened,
waiting for another attack
only to find out the next day
that a businessman
had electrocuted himself
on the power lines
with a kite.

Evolution
(as recorded by an innocent alien bystander)

From water to land,
from air to land,
from ape to woman
and man, who soon learned

to use their tools
and learned to create
before there were rules,
before there were dates.

Soon they learned to speak
and then how to write
but things still looked bleak—
they never learned right.

Then they made laws,
then they made books,
something called religion,
then they made hooks

to hang the weak
who would not agree.

Wars were fought,
lives were lost,
blood was spilled
for good and for worse.

They took new land,
they killed the Buffalo,
they planted a seed

and watched steel and glass grow.

They built great machines
of science and greed
and returned to where they began
when it all blew up in their faces.

Greed for Gold

We set out on journeys
Modern day explorers
With nowhere new to go
Except the past.
So we retrace steps
Backwards in time
Where machines, buildings, and highways
disappear
Where trees spring up
And we pull the arrows from our chests
And walk past gold without a thought.
The waves of blood turn to water
The sky is crisp and blue again
The ground fertile and green
Becomes our dance floor once more

For the great ghost dance

To restore peace and faith
In a place where we don't suffer
From a disease of the heart

Of which only gold can cure.

Looking to the Future

From the big bang to artificial intelligence
What a cosmological stretch eventually leading
To the evolution of a burgeoning black hole—
We're probably already half way there
Starting with the greenhouse effect,
A nuclear winter of sorts looming—
Quakes, hurricanes, tornadoes, rising sea levels.
What's the cure for this one?

Adam Swallowed

Crimson flowers that yield sleep-like death
to the sweating dizzy person down
on the ground where the wild boar roams
sniffing, licking your tears from your face.
The boar decides to leave you be
and not eat you, as you might do to him,
but the hungry snake is sure to disagree
and feast on you one limb at a time
until you are swallowed whole
in the belly of a garden behemoth
swelling in the darkness within
that shiny skin your feet once wore.

Sense

Where is there a trace of decency
In this world? You ask
When I show you the film
Of a man beheading a pig
With a chainsaw
Laughing
For kicks.
Fire in the man's eyes
As the pig's body jumps about
Proving that the body still feels
After it is separated from the head
And that animals do in fact feel
And some humans indeed do not.

Pangs Of…

Do you know the path I follow?
The one with long winding passages
Up rocky hillsides
Down into blood-soaked valleys
Through villages plagued by genocide
Over bodies left for dead
Flies buzzing
Mothers crying
Whips cracking
Chains dangling
Past a plantation of capitalism
Through windows of disease factories
And a white house of corporatism
And through the big blinding cities
Where everyone's eyes are glued in front
Ahead and above, your stare
But below the truth that blows in the wind
Back to the suburbs
Where comfort matters the most
Right through your front door
On your TV
On your table
In your sick mouth
Through your intestines
And I never really come out
That stubborn vengeance
And vicious cycle
Of perpetual war
Every single day
Every single time you pick up a fork
Say a prayer
And eat a soul.

Bite and Run

Someday I'm going to break out of this chain
Run free
Through the country
Stop to lie in the sun
Roll on the grass
Lick the wounds of my past.

For now I sit in the dirt
Beaten
Broken
Wanting to bite him in the face
Every time he kicks me
Or leaves me out in the rain
Or even just looks at me
With his ugly grimace

But I know if I bite him
And fail to kill
I'd be doomed for sure.
He'd be certain to get out the rifle
And then bury me in the back
Cursing as he shoveled and bled
In the dirt I now inhabit.

Knowing he occasionally brings me in
I'll just keep waiting
For that single moment
The collar slips
Just enough from his grasp.

Ideas

Concrete
A sledgehammer falls
Dust is left
To blow on
Farther into the world
For the wind to steal away
The bones of yesterday.
Some of them off to other lands
To land on homes and schools
To slowly colonize a new world.
Others off to the oceans
Food for whales and fish
To mix with the blood of the Earth
To be cleansed of life.

Fractions

Humans have already been there.
And we built roads and condos,
Factories and power plants,
Now there's only a small fraction of heaven left.

Survey

Are You?
- ☐ Aware and awake
- ☐ Sleepwalking 9-5
- ☐ Living for the moment
- ☐ Already a corpse

Where do you live?
- ☐ In a smoggy city
- ☐ In a pretty beige home
- ☐ On a farm
- ☐ Nowhere but everywhere

Do you feel?
- ☐ Nothing
- ☐ Excruciating pain
- ☐ Exhilarating bliss
- ☐ Universal empathy

What do you hear?
- ☐ Birds
- ☐ Traffic
- ☐ A train rumbling along the tracks
- ☐ Silence

Do you smell?
- ☐ War
- ☐ Flowers
- ☐ Death on a grill
- ☐ Ocean breeze

Who are you?
- ☐ A pessimist
- ☐ A realist
- ☐ An optimist
- ☐ _____

ABOUT THE AUTHOR

Once upon a time, WK Lawrence was a punk. For this bio, he didn't think it mattered where he was born, or where he grew up, or where he lives now. He also didn't think it was important to boast where he went to college. He certainly didn't think it was appropriate to list his publications. His website can be found somewhere online. Sometimes there's a little bit of a punk still left in him. He is the author of the novel titled *The Punk and the Professor*.

Printed in Great Britain
by Amazon

22526444R00061